# SPITFIRE

# SPITFIRE

## The World's Most Famous Fighter

**JEREMY FLACK**

BB **Bounty**
BOOKS

First published in 1985 by Osprey Publishing
Reprinted in 1994 by Chancellor Press (Bounty Books)

This edition published in 2015 by Bounty Books,
a division of Octopus Publishing Group Ltd,
Carmelite House
50 Victoria Embankment
London, EC4Y 0DZ

An Hachette UK Company
www.hachette.co.uk

ISBN: 978-0-753729-77-9

A CIP catalogue record for this book is available from the British
Library

Printed and bound in China

10 9 8 7 6 5 4 3 2 1

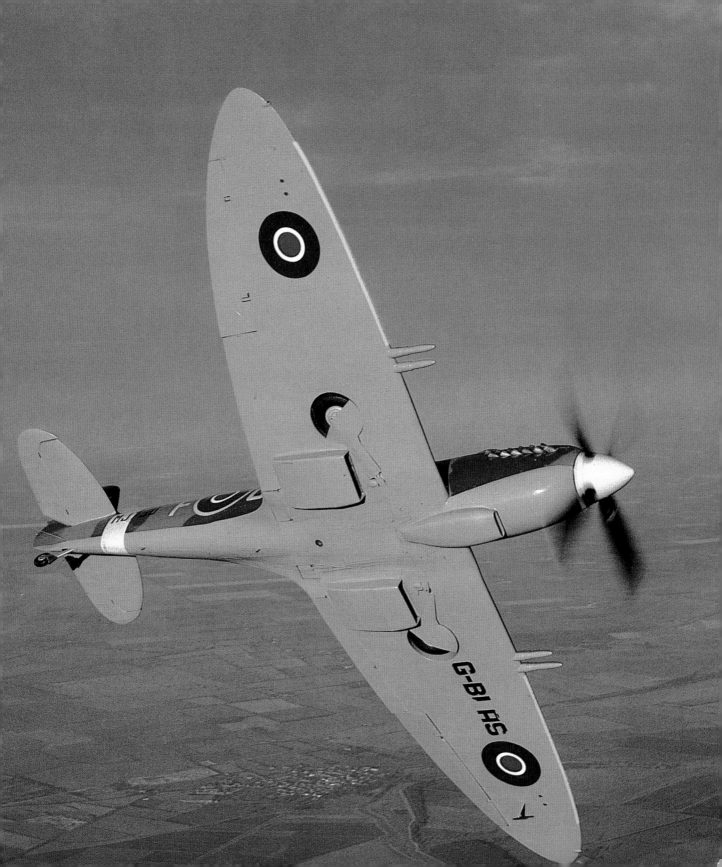

# Wing leader

Originally delivered as a Spitfire LF Mk IX (Merlin 66), MH434/G-ASJV is now powered by a Merlin 76, a right-hand tractor unit from a de Havilland Mosquito. The engine has a maximum continuous rating of 1375 hp (2850 rpm + 12 lb of boost) at an altitude of 13,500 ft, consuming 100L avgas at the rate of 150 gallons per hour.

MH434 was one of 5095 Mk IXs built at the Castle Bromwich Aircraft Factory (CBAF) and it entered service with No 222 (Natal) Sqn in 1943. During its career with this unit the aircraft was credited with two Fw 190s destroyed, and a shared kill on a Bf 109F. It

saw further action after WW II with the Royal Netherlands Air Force in Indonesia. Today, MH434 wears No 222 Sqn codes again and the machine is operated by The Old Flying Machine Company from Duxford Airfield. **Left** Mark Hanna nears the top of a loop. **Below** Holding formation on a P-51D Mustang when MH434 sported the initials of its former owner Adrian Swire. **Overleaf** Mark Hanna's father, Ray, is flying the Curtiss P-40E Kittyhawk owned by John Paul of Alamo, California. Codes 'SU-E' spell out the first name of Paul's wife

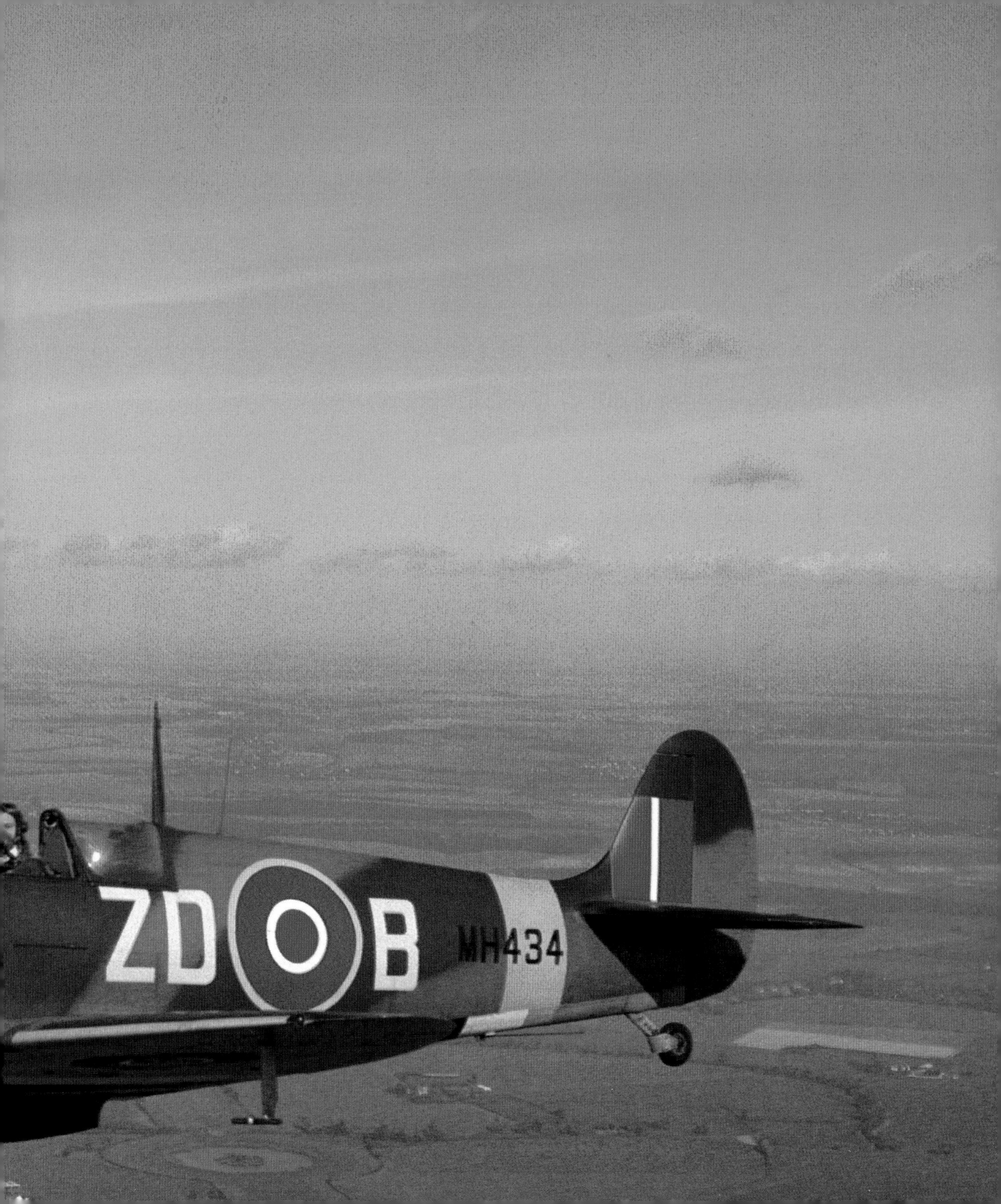
ZD B
MH434

**Preceding pages and left** Mark Hanna flying an aerobatic sequence in MH434. A positive loading of 5G must never be exceeded. **Below** Fast and low in the Hanna tradition. **Overleaf** Making angels

Spitfire F Mk XIV owned by Rolls-Royce Ltd and based at Castle Donington near Derby. RM689/G-ALGT has accumulated only 1000 flying hours. Its Griffon 65 engine delivers 2050 hp at 2750 rpm and +12 lb of boost. Purists will point out that despite being coded 'AP-D', this Spitfire never served with No 130 Sqn. But isn't the sight and sound of its airborne majesty more important? **Right and overleaf** G-FIRE has been transformed since it was re-discovered with its outer wings hacked off in a Belgian scrap yard and bought for £250. A variety of owners and £100,000 later (spent by Spencer Flack),

Spitfire FR Mk XIVe (NH904) is now resplendant in striking scarlet. The restoration was handled by Mike Searle at Ambrion Aviation, Elstree. G-FIRE is now owned by the Classic Air Displays syndicate, also based at Elstree. For the lat shot in the following sequence, pilot Ken Whitehead uses only a whisker of power from G-FIRE's 2050 horse Griffon 65 to 'loose deuce' with Mike Searle's half-scale WAR Fw 190 replica adorned in II/JG 1 'Oesau' warpaint.

**Page 26/27 and inset** Clipped-wing Spitfire LF Mk Vc (AR501/G-AWII) is owned by the Shuttleworth Collection. It was built by Westland Aircraft, issued to No 310 (Czech) Sqn in July 1942, and assigned to Sqn Ldr F. Dolezal, DFC. When the aircraft was flown by the late Neil Williams in 1975 after two years of painstaking restoration, it was authentically repainted in its original markings. At the time of writing, AR510 is grounded after severe corrosion was discovered in the root of a propeller blade. Clipping the wing improved its geometric efficiency, increasing speed and the rate of roll at low level to combat the Bf 109F. But the extra induced drag and loss of lift had a negative effect on landing and take-off run, range, and ceiling

**Preceding page, this page, and overleaf** Aldermaston is better known today for nuclear weapon research and the design and manufacture of nuclear warheads, but in 1945 Spitfire FR Mk XIV NH749 emerged from the Aldermaston works of Vickers-Armstrongs. After NH749 was despatched to Karachi, India, in July 1945, its history with the Indian Air Force is extremely difficult to decipher. However, the late Ormond Haydon-Baillie brought it back to England in 1978 where it was re-sold to A. and K. Wickenden and subsequently registered as G-MXIV on 11 April 1980. By 1983 the aircraft had been restored to flying condition by Keith Wickenden and it was offered for sale at Christie's aircraft auction at Duxford, but a final bid of £180,000 failed to attain the reserve price. Sadly, Keith Wickenden died in a flying accident and G-MXIV will probably be sold in the near future

**This page and overleaf** Frenchman Roland Fraissinet is the owner of this Spitfire PR Mk XI (PL983/G-PRXI) which was impeccably restored to airworthiness by Phillip Tillyard of Trent Aero Engineering, based at East Midlands Airport (Castle Donington.) The aircraft is painted in the PRU Blue scheme used by No 4 Sqn, 2nd Tactical Air Force (TAF).

Speed meant survival in the photo reconnaissance business, every precious knot of airspeed reducing the risk of interception by enemy fighters—a Merlin-70 powered PR Mk XI was capable of 422 mph at 27,000 ft. Different types of cameras and lenses were carried to suit the particular requirements of each mission; options included F.8 cameras (20 inch focal length), F.24s (14 inch focal length), and F.52s (36 inch focal length.) Obliquely-mounted cameras in blister fairings could also be fitted outboard of each wheel well under the wing.

G-PRXI normally lives at Castle Donington and is expected to participate in a number of air shows across Western Europe. During a sojourn in France at the end of 1984, the aircraft was flown from Istres by no less a pilot than Mirage master Jean Marie Saget. The jockey on this occasion is Mike Searle

**Preceding page** 'Missing man' formation of Spitfires over the International Air Tattoo at Greenham Common in 1983 paid tribute to the memory of Sir Douglas Bader, the famous WW II fighter ace. **Above and right** Spitfire LF Mk IXe (ML417) owned by Stephen Grey departs from Kemble where the paint job was completed. **Overleaf** Spitfire Mk II (P7350) of the Battle of Britain Memorial Flight over the hedge on finals to land. It has since been re-coded 'SH-D'

# Spits in pieces: restoring a legend

The restoration and servicing of old aeroplanes is a difficult, time-consuming process, but Booker-based Personal Plane Services are more than equal to the task. Edna and Tony Bianchi are the power behind the company, formed in 1947 by the late Doug Bianchi and now busier than ever. **Left and bottom right** Stephen Grey's LF Mk IXe (ML417/G-BJSG) in primer is a born again single-seat Spitfire. Re-converting the aircraft from a T Mk 9 trainer involved re-siting the front cockpit 13 inches aft and many of the frames had to be built from scratch; areas of fuselage, wings, and tail were re-skinned. **Top right** Packed PPS hangar includes a fully painted ML417, a French-built Morane MS.500 (Fieseler Storch), and Kermit Weeks' Mosquito

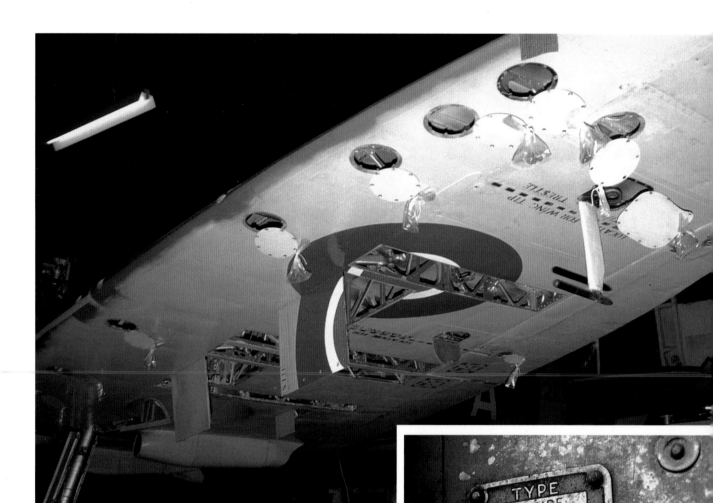

No shortage of access panels on the wing of Spitfire Mk Ia AR213. **Inset** Mod plate of Spitfire LF Mk IXe TE517 reveals that this was the 558th Mk IX built by the Castle Bromwich Aircraft Factory (CBAF.) **Top right** Engine bearer struts of Mk Ia AR213. **Below** When its engine was pulled the c/n plate of the Heston Aircraft Company emerged from behind a coat of paint

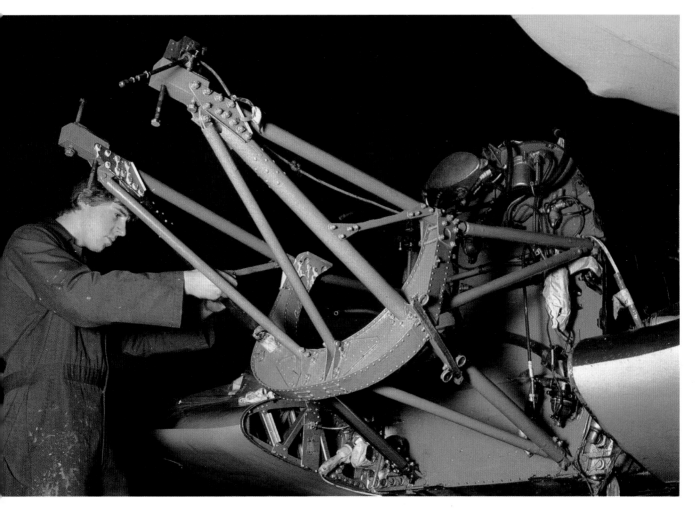

Spitfire LF Mk IX (TE517/G-BIXP) will be rebuilt to flying condition under the guidance of Dick Melton at Vintage Airworks, St Leonards-on-Sea. **Opposite page** The fuselage interior is grubby but the frames are in a satisfactory state. TE517 was sold to Israel in 1949 after serving in the advanced training role with the Czech Air Force. It was eventually recovered from a kibbutz near Gaaton in 1977. **Right** The wings are being restored by Trent Aero Engineering. **Above right** Connecting the hydraulics of the retractable tailwheel fitted to PR Mk XI PL983

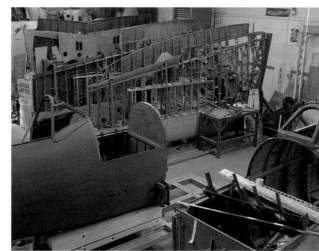

49

Spitfire LF Mk IXe (TE566/G-BLCK) owned by
Steve Atkins at Vintage Airworks swops old skin for
new metal. **Right** Spitfire Mk IX (MJ730/G-BLAS)
nearing completion. **Opposite and overleaf** Spitfire
PR Mk XI PL983 being re-assembled by Trent Aero
Engineering in Rolls-Royce's hangar at East Midlands
Airport. Mk XIV RM689 in the foreground (overleaf)

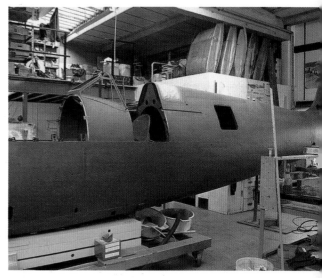

Structurally complete, the exterior of Spitfire PR Mk XI PL983 is carefully prepared and primed to obtain a high standard of finish. Inaccessible areas are sprayed before final assembly. **Above** The elevators and hinge control are presented to the fin and tailplane

Spray gunner gives a coat of PRU Blue to PL983.
**Right** The spinner and backplate are blue, too

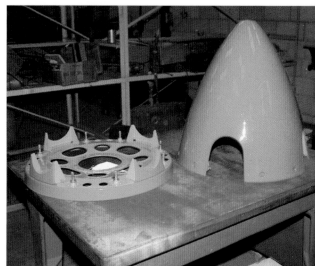

Spitfire LF Mk IXe ML417 being refuelled before a test flight. **Left** Internal and external attention. **Overleaf, left** Biggles' flies undone? Tony Bianchi confers with his team after an engine run. **Overleaf, right** The cockpit comes with all mod comms

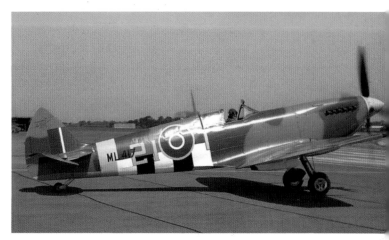

ML417's Packard Merlin 266 running cleanly before and after the camouflage and markings were applied. The codes belong to No 443 (RCAF) Sqn, 2nd TAF, circa June 1944

**Preceding page** Immac Spitfire PR Mk XI PL983 taxies out for take-off at Castle Donington in the summer of '84. **Inset** Its Packard Merlin 266 was purchased from Jack Hovey and shipped from the States. Phillip Tillyard (right) keeps a watchful eye on the engine as it fires up in the airframe for the first time. **Above** Turnin' and burnin' at Duxford. **Right** Extra ballast is required to hold the tail down with the throttle wide open

# A Spitfire built for two

During WW II the demand for Spitfire fighters was enormous (more than 20,000 were built in two dozen major marks) and no production capacity was allocated to two-seat trainer versions. After the war about 20 airframes were bastardized from existing Mk IXs and exported to a small number of air forces. T Mk 9 ML407/G-LFIX (below) started life at Castle Bromwich as an LF Mk IXc and saw operational service with No 485 (RNZAF) Sqn from April 1944 until January 1945. After conversion by Vickers, ML407 was sold to the Irish Air Corps in 1951 and operated from Baldonnel as IAC162 until its retirement in 1960. Nick Grace acquired the aircraft in 1979 and has completed a five year restoration at St Merryn, Cornwall, for the British Aviation Heritage

**Left** Fitting and wiring the instruments in the front cockpit prior to installing the main upper fuel tank.
**Overleaf** The front (left) and rear cockpits of G-LFIX. Large spade grip on the stick was hinged for lateral control, while the whole column moved fore and aft for pitch imputs

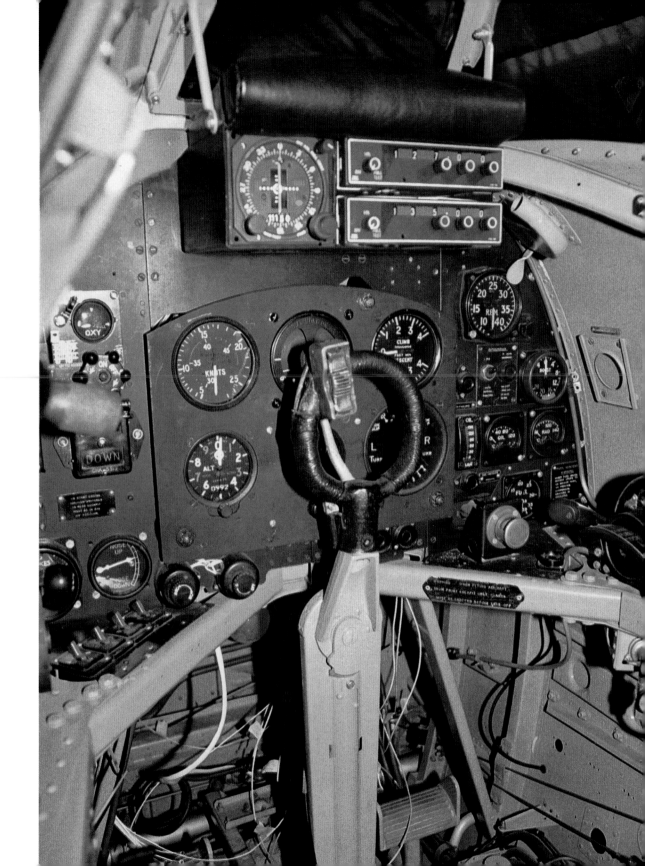

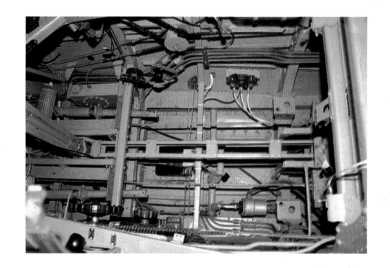

Left Two-seat configuration looks strange. Fuel lines, control wires, and electrics are installed underneath the wing root fillet, or (right) along the bottom of fuselage under the pilots' seat. **Below** The Merlin 25 fitted to G-LFIX. **Overleaf** 'Spitfires do taxi in IMC'. In fact the smoke screen is the result of 30 years of inhibitor being blasted out of the Merlin's 12 cylinders. **Inset** Nick Grace and his wife, Carolyn, see clearly now the engine is running sweetly. **Page 74/75** G-AIDN in a variety of colour schemes. After a landing mishap at Coventry in 1978, the aircraft has remained in storage

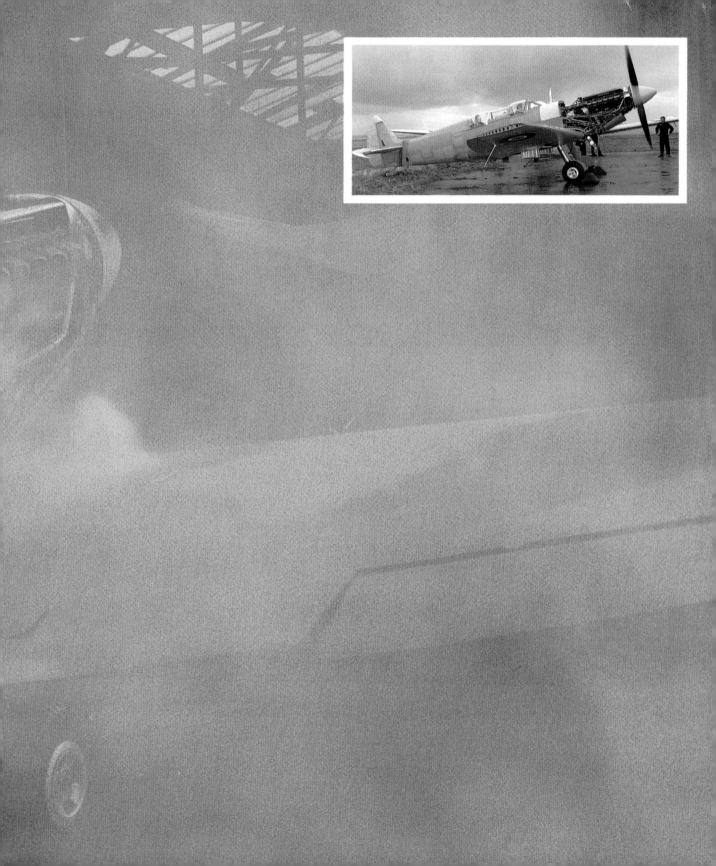

# Battle of Britain Memorial Flight

The BBMF was formed at Biggin Hill on 11 July 1957 to commemorate the major battle honour of the Royal Air Force, won against the *Luftwaffe* in the summer of 1940. **Below** Spitfire Mk II P7350 has served with the flight since October 1968. 'SH-D' (No 64 Sqn codes) is powered by a Merlin 35. **Right** Spitfire LF Mk Vb AB910 suffered appalling damage in August 1978 during an air show at Bex, Switzerland, when a Harvard chewed into it on the ground after swinging on take-off. After incredible repair work at Abingdon, the aircraft was returned to the flight, fully serviceable, on 26 October 1981. Strengthening plates on the wing (below right) are a visible legacy of the collision

**Left, inset, and overleaf** Spitfire PR Mk XIX PM631 is one of the original members of the BBMF. As part of the RAF's contribution to the 40th anniversary of D-Day, the aircraft was repainted in full invasion stripery as 'DL-E' of No 91 Sqn, circa June 1944. Interestingly, at the time of the Indonesian Confrontation in 1964, PM631 took part in dogfighting exercises with the supersonic English Electric Lightning interceptor, just in case the RAF was forced to mix it with Indonesian Air Force P-51 Mustangs—a somewhat extreme example of dissimilar air combat training

**Preceding page** Not a rare colour photograph of a wartime MU (maintenance unit), but the interior of the BBMF hangar at Coningsby, Lincolnshire, in December 1984. Four Spits, a Hurricane, and the world's only airworthy Lancaster bomber are being serviced. **Below** Spitfire LF Mk Vb AB910, this time in the earlier 'QJ-J' codes used by Jeffrey Quill. He flew during the Battle of Britain with No 92 Sqn during a 'break' from test flying the Spitfire. The aircraft is on jacks at No 5 MU at Kemble following a landing gear collapse at Duxford in June 1976—the damage was made good by 21 December. An Andover (perhaps better known in its civil guise as the 748) is in the background. **Right** Spitfire PR Mk XIX PS853 being modified to accept a Griffon 58 (ex-Shackleton.) A windfall of Griffon engines has been delayed by problems with the replacement for the Shackleton airborne early warning (AEW) aircraft, the BAe Nimrod AEW.3

# Spitfires, Spit fliers

Mark (in cockpit) and Ray Hanna with Spitfire Mk IX MH434 consult each other before their display slots. **Below** Mark Hanna is normally an F-4 driver in the RAF, but looks equally at home in a Spitfire

**Preceding page and above** Spitfire spectacular at
West Malling attracted Mk XIV G-FIRE, Mk XIV
NH749/'L', Mk IX MH434/'ZD-B', Mk Ia
AR213/'QG-A', LF Mk Vb AB910/'XT-M' and
Hawker Hurricane Mk IIc PZ865 *The Last of the
Many*, the final example built, sneaks in at the end.
Hurricane production ceased in August 1944 at number
14,231, just as Spitfire output peaked at 500 per month.
**Overleaf** Cherokee 140 serves to emphasize the
beautifully proportioned lines of the Spitfire Mk XIV.
NH749 is based at the Cranfield College of Aeronautics
and students are happy to have their lectures
interrupted when Angus McVitie (inset) takes her for
a test flight

**Preceding page** The chocks are pulled away from MH434 at North Weald. **Inset** Ray Hanna chatting to engineer Roger Shepherd, the man responsible for keeping the aircraft serviceable. **Left** The Honourable Patrick Lindsay's Spitfire Mk Ia (AR213/G-AIST) parked at Alconbury. **Below** Sitting pretty at North Weald in 1984: the groundcrew relax on the grass underneath MH434, recreating a timeless image repeated at many Spitfire dispersals during WW II. **Overleaf** Spitfire LF Mk IXc NH238 seems to have got it a bit rich

**Preceding page with insets** NH238/G-MKIX is one of the many Spitfires acquired by Doug Arnold of Warbirds of Great Britain. Presently based at Blackbushe, the aircraft is expected to move to Bitteswell with the rest of his warbird collection. G-MKIX was formerly resident in the States as N238V, painted to represent the Spitfire Mk IX 'JE-J' flown by wing leader Johnny Johnson, and used to score the majority of his 38 kills. **Top left** Wg Cdr 'Dicky' Martin in the cockpit of the Shuttleworth Collection's LF Mk Vc. **Bottom left** Spitfire Mk Vb BL614 has

been one of the star attractions of the Manchester Air & Space Museum since 1982. Unlike the airworthy Mk Vs, BL614 is fitted with the correct exhaust stubs common to Merlin-engined Spitfires until the introduction of the Merlin 60 series in the marks VII, VIII, and IX with individual ejectors. The aircraft has been restored to No 222 (Natal) Sqn codes 'ZD-F' which it wore when the RAF provided air cover for the bloody Dieppe raid in August 1942. **Above** Mike Searle poses in PR Mk XI PL983

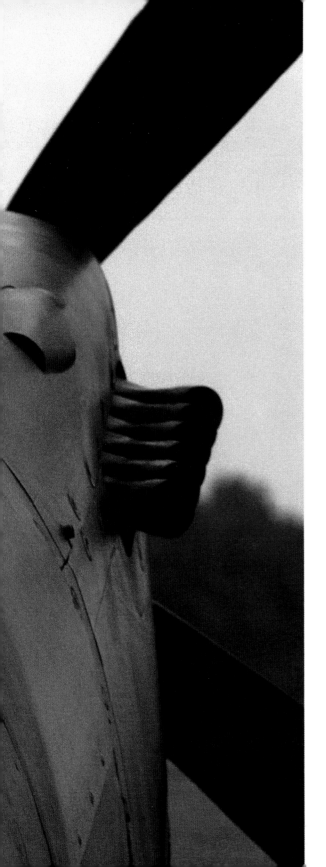

# Spit bits

The Spitfire's long snout plus tail-dragger undercarriage equals practically zero forward visibility. Weaving is essential to avoid expensive noises up front when you are manoeuvring on the ground. This is a Merlin-powered Spitfire Mk IX (MH434). Staying with the subject of visibility, until the cut down rear fuselage and 360-degree vision canopy were introduced a rear view mirror helped to check six and spot the bad guy curving in behind you. **Below** To prevent moisture being sucked into the engine as it cools off, disposable plastic cups are stuffed up the exhaust manifold exit pipes

**Left** Dave Reader tops up the oil tank of MH434 with Aeroshell W120; its Merlin 76 drinks 34 pints an hour at maximum continuous power. **Above** 'Sir, is one bidding or just picking one's nose? *Thank you*'. Gavel in hand, Spitfire owner and pilot, The Honourable Patrick Lindsay, officiates at Christie's aircraft sale at Duxford Airfield in 1984. A final bid of a cool £320,000 failed to meet the reserve price set for Roland Fraissinet's PR Mk XI. In the background a de Havilland Tiger Moth and a Dragon Rapide look on. Any offers? **Overleaf** The trolley-acc is pulled away after injecting 12 volts AC into the starter motor circuit of Shuttleworth's LF Mk Vc at Old Warden. **Page 110/111** German Hoffmann prop gives G-FIRE pulling power

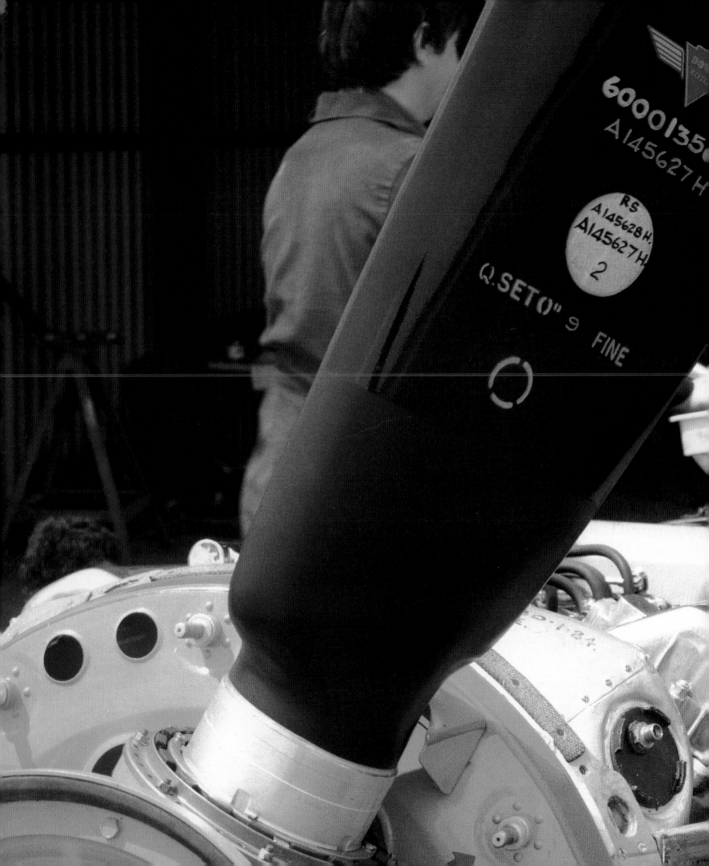

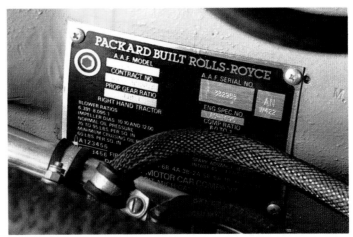

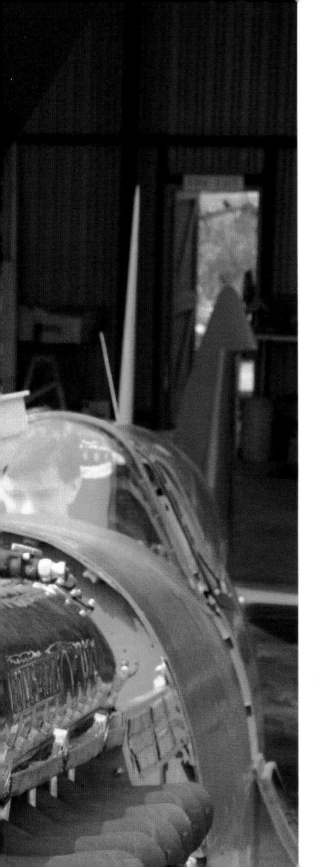

**Left** Zero-houred Dowty Rotol propeller fitted to PR Mk XI PL983 complete with logo. **Top** Oil-cooler intake of LF Mk Vc AR501, mounted under the left wing. **Middle** Merlin production was augmented by Packard who built the engine under license in America. **Bottom** Carburettor air intake duct under the nose of LF Mk Vc AR501

**Left** Flashing strobe lights in the muzzles of G-FIRE's Hispanos are a big hit at air shows. **Bottom left** Gun camera port in the left wing root of LF Mk Vc AR501. **Bottom right** Wing strengthening and cannon fairing (introduced because of the size of the ammunition feed drum for the 20 mm Hispano) of LF Mk Vc AR501

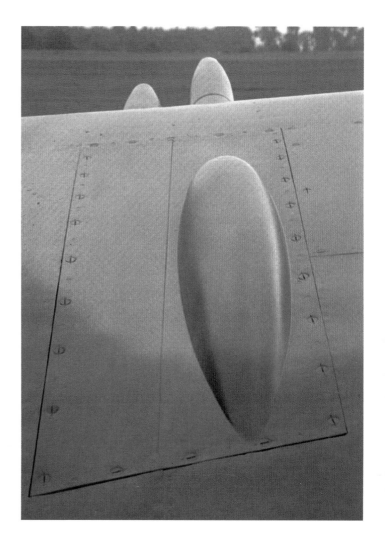

**This page, right and bottom right** Hispano armament of LF Mk IXe ML417 indicates the provision for two additional cannons shown by the inboard stubs and space for a second fairing on the wing. If the two extra cannons were fitted, the four 0.303 Browning machine guns were deleted. **Below** Hispano installation on LF Mk Vc with cannon barrel fairing

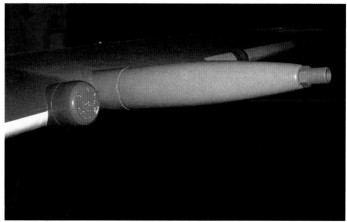

Spitting image? John Isaccs' 6/10ths scale Spitfire replica G-BBJI is powered by a 100 hp Continental O-200 flat-four engine giving a maximum speed of 150 mph. Fully aerobatic, its wooden airframe is stressed to a healthy +9/4·5G; the landing gear is non-retractable. Before he became a school master John Isaccs was employed by Vickers at their Woolston works near Southampton Water and was closely involved in Spitfire production. G-BBJI first flew on 5 May 1975 and was originally painted silver overall, but PRU Blue was the colour of the day at Duxford in 1984. **Right** IFF (Identification Friend or Foe) was already in use by the RAF at the beginning of WW II. Spitfire LF Mk Vc AR501 is probably the only example with a pair of authentic aerials. **Extreme right** Dr Gordon Mitchell, the son of Spitfire designer R. J. Mitchell, in front of Spitfire PR Mk XI PL983

117

Clive Du Cros is building this full-size flying replica of the prototype Spitfire K5054 in a secret location somewhere in Swindon. Nicknamed the 'wooden wonder', it is being constructed using douglas fir and sitka spruce covered by birch ply. Power will be provided by the specially modified Jaguar V12 automobile engine on the right. Du Cros aims to have the aeroplane ready for the 50th anniversary of the Spitfire's maiden flight, the historic event which took place at Eastleigh near Southampton when Capt J. 'Mutt' Summers, Vickers' chief test pilot, pulled back on the stick of K5054 on 5 March 1936. Unlike the original, the replica will probably have a tailwheel instead of a skid, the modified rudder with smaller horn balance, and fairings for the landing gear from the start. The *real* K5054 was written off after a landing accident at Farnborough on 4 September 1939

The normal and emergency landing gear ('chassis')
operating controls. **Overleaf** Mark Hanna's leather
flying helmet and mask ready for another air show
scramble in MH434

119

# 'First of the Few'

5 March 1936. The prototype Supermarine Type 300 K5054, as yet unnamed, awaits its first flight from the Supermarine Aviation Works at Eastleigh Airport near Southampton ... Not quite. 55 years separate this photograph from the day Reginald Mitchell's masterpiece took to the air, for this is Clive du Cros's magnificent full-scale replica of the first Spitfire, awaiting *its* maiden flight in the summer of 1991 at RAF Hullavington in Wiltshire

**Right and opposite** Unlike the original, du Cros's prototype Spitfire is made entirely from wood, a douglas fir and sitka spruce airframe skinned with birch ply, but is otherwise faithful to the clean unspoilt lines of the original

No Merlin this, but a Jaguar V-12 automobile engine with modified fuel and oil systems and dual ignition. Capacity has been increased to six litres, enabling the engine to put out 350 hp via a custom-built reduction gearbox. The Type 300's Merlin C produced close to its design power output of 1000 hp

Clive, son Christian and many willing helpers were on hand to move the replica from its workshop in Swindon to the gliding club hangar at RAF Hullavington where final assembly took place

With most systems installed, first engine runs were made on 13 February 1990, followed by 25 hours of ground trials which included high speed runs down Hullavington's main runway. The silver dope paint scheme of du Cros's replica duplicates the natural metal and primer finish in which the real K5054 made its initial flight before being given a high gloss finish of Supermarine Seaplane Enamel, the precise bluish-grey shade of which is the subject of endless debate among latter-day researchers

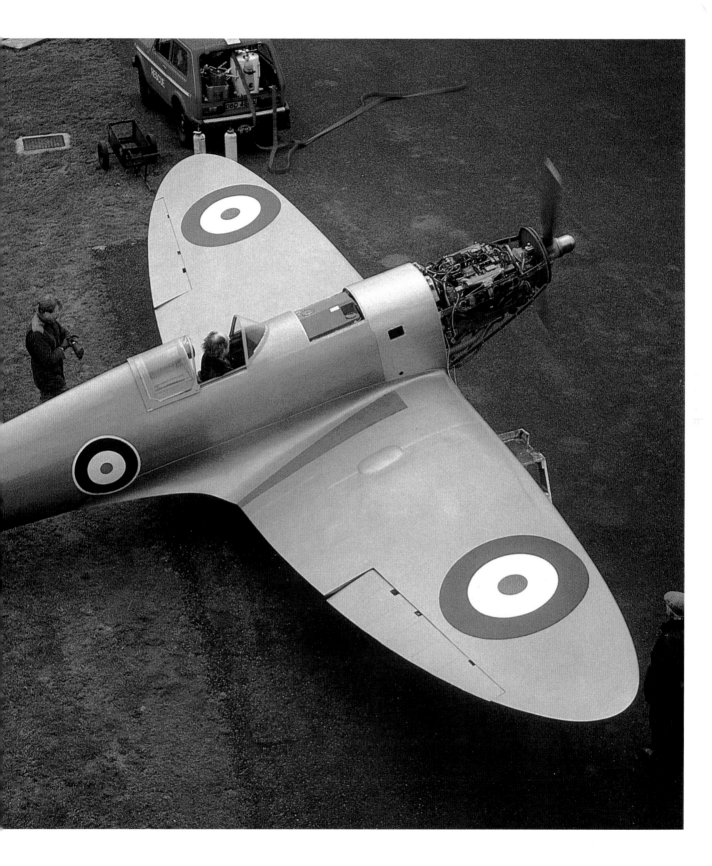

Once preliminary trials of the Jaguar V-12 were satisfactorily completed, Clive was ready to install the Spitfire's close-fitting cowling panels. Slotted wheel hubs, large underwing radiator fairing, round rather than oval exhaust ports and (not seen here) a tailwheel rather than a skid are concessions to total authenticity, but lack of undercarriage leg fairings is correct – they were not fitted to K5054 until after its first flight

**Above** Test pilot Pete Thorn studies the instrument panel layout with engineer Nick Pearson prior to the first flight. Although the basic flight instruments are identical to those of the original Spitfire, engine gauges reflect the Jaguar's automobile ancestry

**Right** She flies! Pete Thorn lifts the 'second' K5054 off Hullavington's runway on 7 June 1991, two days after the 55th anniversary of the original's maiden flight, and the culmination of 10 years' hard work for Clive du Cros and his team. Apocryphal story has it that after Vickers test pilot 'Mutt' Summers flew the type 300 for just 15 minutes on that day in 1936 he declared it perfect, a real 'flies off the drawing board' aeroplane. Of such stuff are legends made, but, alas, rarely are they true. Summers' protégé Jeffrey Quill, who was at Eastleigh for the first flight and, after Summers' retirement, became the doyen of Spitfire test pilots, recalls that what Summers actually said to designer Reginald Mitchell was that he didn't want anything touched or altered until he had a chance to fly K5054 again and assess it more thoroughly – not quite the same thing. Mitchell never lived to see the Spitfire enter service or develop through its myriad of different versions far removed from the design he had conceived; he died of stomach cancer a year after K5054 flew. Nor did the prototype last long. Brought up to production Mk I standard, it overturned on landing, killing its pilot, at Farnborough on 4 September 1939 – the day after war was declared. The historic airframe, which had logged just over 151 flying hours, was briefly used as a mock-up for photo reconnaissance camera installations and then scrapped

# Up where they belong

**These pages and overleaf** Closer . . . closer . . . hold it! Sqn Ldr Paul Day, AFC, Fighter Leader of the RAF's Battle of Britain Memorial Flight, tucks Spitfire PR Mk XIX PM631 ever tighter into the lens. One of three PR Mk XIXs in the BBMF's collection of five Spitfires, PM631 is the only one not to have seen wartime service. Built at Reading in late 1945, it spent most of its early years with Maintenance Units before joining the Meteorological Research Flight at Hooton Park in 1951, and was a founder member of the BBMF when it formed at RAF Biggin Hill in July 1957. On the Flight's strength ever since, PM631 spent some time at RAF Binbrook in 1963 in the unlikely role of dissimilar air combat 'aggressor', flying against English Electric Lightnings of the Central Fighter Establishment at a time when it was thought possible that RAF Lightnings might be pitted against North American P-51D Mustangs during the Indonesian Confrontation

**Above** Then, and now. In 1985 AVM Ken Hayr, AOC No 11 Group, Strike Command, came up with the novel idea of teaming one of the RAF's oldest fighters with its latest interceptor for a unique airshow routine. Fortuitously No 229 OCU, then converting onto the Panavia F.2 Tornado, and the Battle of Britain Memorial Flight, shared a common base at RAF Coningsby, Lincolnshire. Here Sqn Ldr Paul Day, himself a No 229 OCU instructor, leads the 'Spitnado' duo in PM631 while Wg Cdr Rick Peacock-Edwards holds station in the F.2, wings at full forward sweep and slats extended

**Right** Photo reconnaissance was an important role for Spitfires during World War 2. The PR Mk XIX was the last of the PR marks, combining the high back fuselage, 2035 hp Rolls-Royce Griffon 66 engine and tail surfaces of the FR Mk XIV, modified PR Mk XI wings and its universal camera installation, and the pressurised cockpit of the PR Mk X. It had a maximum speed of 445 mph at 26,000 feet, a service ceiling of more than 42,000 feet and, with internal fuel capacity of 252 gallons (treble that of the Battle of Britain era Mk I) and 90- or 170-gallon drop tanks, could range more than 1400 miles. A total of 225 PR Mk XIXs were built. After World War 2 the Swedish Air Force purchased 50 PR Mk XIXs, while others went to India and Thailand. Here PM631 wears late war camouflage and black-and-white invasion stripes to masquerade as Mk XIV DL-E of No 91 Sqn for the 40th anniversary of the D-Day landings in 1984

**This page and overleaf** Though less than a wingspan separates these two Spitfires, they represent opposite ends of the development spectrum. On the left, the BBMF's Mk IIA P7350 is the oldest aircraft in the Flight, dating from September 1940, while PR Mk XIX PM631 was a post-war baby, sharing little in common with its progenitor save for the name. Compare 'clean' wing, curved frameless windscreen and long nose of the Griffon-engined PR Mk XIX with eight-gun wing (red-doped patches were to prevent cold air freezing up the unfired guns at altitude), armoured glass windscreen and early model Merlin front end of the Mk IIA as they run in at low level for a flypast during an International Air Tattoo at RAF Fairford

**Preceding pages** Puffy white clouds and a Spitfire in which to chase them. What more could any man ask?

**These pages** Gleaming in the high gloss PRU Blue finish it wore while serving with No 16 Sqn, 2nd Tactical Air Force in 1945, PS853 is another of the Battle of Britain Memorial Flight's trio of Spitfire PR Mk XIXs. Built at Supermarine's Southampton works, it entered service with the Central Photographic Reconnaissance unit at RAF Benson, Oxfordshire in January 1945 and saw action with 2TAF in Belgium, the Netherlands and Germany. Like BBMF companions PM631 and PS915, '853 ended its active service with the celebrated Met Flight at Hooton Park and RAF Woodvale on THUM (Temperature and Humidity) duties, and made the RAF' last ever Spitfire operational sortie on 9 June 1957, following which the THUM task was taken over by DH Mosquitoes. Four days later Group Captain Johnnie Johnson ferried the aircraft to Biggin Hill to join the newly established Memorial Flight. PS853 was later placed 'on the gate' at Central Fighter Establishment, RAF West Raynham, before restoration to airworthiness for the BBMF in 1964

Shot from the tail-gunner's turret of the BBMF's flagship Avro Lancaster *City of Lincoln*, PR Mk XIX PS853 leads the Flight's Hawker Hurricane IIC LF363, which was the last Hurricane to enter RAF service. Ironically Sqn Ldr Allan Martin, at the helm of PS853 on this occasion, was flying the Hurricane in September 1991 when it suffered an inflight engine failure while en route from the Flight's base at RAF Coningsby to Jersey for a Battle of Britain Week display. Despite Sqn Ldr Martin's skill in making a very rapid wheels-up emergency landing at RAF Wittering, fire quickly consumed the historic airframe. Though not completely destroyed, its future is uncertain

...ial. PS853's Griffon 66 ran out of hours in 1984. With no replacement to be had, the Flight, in conjunction with Rolls-Royce, engineered a conversion to enable the more plentiful Griffon 58 from Avro Shackletons to be installed. It flew again, externally unchanged but with much internal redesign and modification, in July 1989

**Above and overleaf** Affectionally known to BBMF members as 'Baby', Mk IIA P7350 was the 14th of 11,939 Spitfires built at Vickers-Armstrong's 'shadow' Castle Bromwich Aircraft Factory (CBAF) near Birmingham. Entering service with No 266 (Rhodesia) Sqn at RAF Wittering on 6 September 1940, it later served with Nos 603 (City of Edinburgh), 616 (County of South Yorkshire) and 4 Sqn and with the Central Gunnery School at RAF Sutton Bridge, and is credited with having destroyed three enemy aircraft (not entirely unscathed – BMF maintenance staff say you can still see bullet hole repair patches in its skin). Repaired three times after suffering Category B damage in flying accidents, P7350 ended its service days with 39 Maintenance Unit at RAF Colerne, where it was sold as scrap for £25. Fortunately the scrap dealer realised the historic value of the aircraft and re-presented it to the station as a museum piece. Restored in 1968, like many other Spitfires, for a role in the epic movie *The Battle of Britain*, the rare Mk IIA was presented to the Battle of Britain Memorial Flight after filming was completed, and is shown here wearing 1985/86 season colours as presentation aircraft *Observer Corps* EB-Z of o 41 Sqn

Aloft from its long-time base at Booker (Wycombe Air Park) is Spitfire Mk IA AR213/G-AIST, which was built by Westland Aircraft at Yeovil in the summer of 1941 as part of a mixed batch of Mks I and V. Already outmoded by later marks, AR213 spent an uneventful war with Operational Training Units and was sold in 1947, along with a Mk V, to Grp Capt (later Air Commodore) Allen Wheeler, and stored unflown with the Shuttleworth Trust at Old Warden Aerodrome until returned to airworthiness as one of the many Spitfire stars of *The Battle of Britain*. The late Hon Patrick Lindsay acquired AR213 and had it maintained in immaculate condition by Personal Plane Services at Booker, whose managing director Tony Bianchi is seen here flying it for current owner Victor Gauntlett, chairman of Proteus Petroleum and a stalwart supporter of historic aircraft preservation and aerobatics in the UK

With her cowling already stained by the exhaust from the Jaguar V-12
powerplant, Clive du Cros's replica of Spitfire prototype K5054 cruises serenely
over the English countryside. Pilot Pete Thorn has slid the canopy back to get a
better view of Jeremy Flack's cameraship

**Left** Them and us. The late Charles Church in his two-seat Spitfire Tr9 PT462/G-CTIX leads his Spanish-built Hispano HA. 1112-M1L Buchon G-HUNN, Swiss Pilatus P-2 G-CJCI – both imitating Messerschmitt Bf 109s with varing degrees of success – and P-51D Mustang G-SUSY on a sortie from his base at Popham, Hampshire

**Opposite** Church's Tr9 started life at Castle Bromwich as a single-seat HF Mk IX. After service with the Mediterranean Allied Air Force it was sold post-war to the Italian Air Force and moved on in 1952 to the Israeli Air Force. Little is known of its career there, but in the early 1980s the partially buried remains of the aircraft were discovered on a kibbutz by British warbirds enthusiast Robs Lamplough and brought back to their homeland after an absence of nearly 40 years. Acquired by Charles Church (Spitfires) Ltd in 1985, PT462 was rebuilt to Supermarine Type 509 Mk 9 Spitfire Trainer configuration by engineer Dick Melton, and flew again for the first time on 25 July 1987 in the hands of Shuttleworth Collection chief pilot John Lewis. Between 1948–51 Vickers converted 20 surplus Mk IX Spitfires to Tr9 standard for export – three for the Dutch Air Force, 10 for the Indian Air Force, one for Egypt and six for the Irish Air Corps

Friend and foe. Spitfire LF Mk XVIE RW382/G-XVIA and Messerschmitt Bf-109G-2/Trop *Black 6*/G-USTV both took to the air again in 1991 after lengthy periods of inactivity. The Spitfire Mk XVI was essentially similar to the Mk IX save for having an American Packard of Detroit-built Merlin 266 instead of a Rolls-Royce engine. RW382 was built in the summer of 1945 and stored for almost two years before being assigned to a squadron. Retired from active service on 14 July 1953 it served as a ground instructional airframe and later as gate guardian of RAF Leconfield, getting its final posting (no pun intended) as a 'pole sitter' at the entrance to RAF Uxbridge in 1973. In 1988, after three years of intense behind-the-scenes negotiation, Cambridge businessman Tim Routsis pulled off the Spitfire restoration coup of all time when he persuaded the British Ministry of Defence to sell him RW382 and four other gate guardian Spitfires for rebuilding to flying condition, in return for providing a dozen highly accurate (and much more weatherproof) glassfibre replica Spitfires and Hurricanes to take their place, and a Bristol Beaufort and Curtiss P-40 for the RAF Museum. Despite its years outdoors RW382 proved to be well-preserved and after a faultlessly authentic restoration by Routsis' company Historic Flying Ltd at Audley End, near Saffron Walden in Essex, it flew again on 3 July 1991, piloted by Air Vice-Marshal John Allison who was in command for this photo session. Wearing the NG-C code letters it carried when assigned to No 604 Sqn Royal Auxiliary Air Force in 1947, the Mk XVIE is owned by American collector David Tallichet (who provided the Beaufort and P-40), but will remain in the UK for the foreseeable future. Routsis and his Historic Flying partner Clive Denney achieved their personal lifetime's ambitions on 7 August 1991 when they both made their first Spitfire solos on the aircraft. And the Messerschmitt? Its *Luftwaffe* career ended two years before RW382 came off the Castle Bromwich production line. Captured by the Royal Australian Air Force in Cyrenaica (now Libya) in 1943, it briefly wore RAAF markings as a CO's personal piece of war booty before being sent to Palestine for evaluation against various marks of Spitfire, and was then shipped to England for comparative trials against contemporary British and American aircraft. Placed in storage in November 1945, it has been the subject of an extraordinarily dedicated 19-year restoration by former RAF Flight Lieutenant Russ Snadden and his volunteer colleagues, culminating in its first flight for 46 years on 17 March 1991. Finished in the authentic *Sandgelb* and *Hellblau* desert camouflage and markings it wore when last flown by Leutnant Heinz Ludemann of 3/JG77, the *Gustav* is the only genuine German-built '109 variant flying anywhere in the world. On loan to the Imperial War Museum and operated from its base at Duxford, Cambridgeshire, it is destined to be retired after three years for permanent (though static) display in the RAF Museum at Hendon. In the meanwhile, AVM Allison, lucky man, flies both RW382 and the *Gustav*, but diplomatically has yet to reveal his preference . . .

The Fighter Collection's Duxford-based Spitfire LF Mk IXE ML417/G-BJSG has a long and interesting pedigree. Built at Castle Bromwich in Birmingham (that famous birthplace of so many Spitfires is now an anonymous council estate) in 1944, it joined No 443 (Royal Canadian Air Force) Sqn and was in action during the D-Day invasion. Based in Normandy immediately after the Allied landings, and later in Belgium, it was credited with two *Luftwaffe* Messerschmitt Bf 109s destroyed and one '109 and a Focke-Wulf Fw 190 damaged/probably destroyed. During 1947/48 ML417 was one of the 20 Mk IXs converted by Vickers to two-seat Tr9 Trainer configuration, and was delivered to the Indian Air Force. Rescued from a storage compound at the IAF Museum in 1971 it journeyed to the USA, then to England for TFC's founder Stephen Grey. Joe Austin and Lawrence Laveris of Personal Plane Services at Booker undertook the task of 'de-trainering' ML417, returning it to original configuration for the third 'first flight' of its lifetime on 29 January 1981. The aircraft has been finished in the carefully-researched colours, No 443 (RCAF) Sqn code 2I-T and invasion identification stripes it wore in 1944, and poignantly returned to the Normandy Beaches on 6 June 1984 to take part in the D-Day 40th anniversary celebration

Another D-Day veteran is Tr9 ML407/G-LFIX, which shared the Castle Bromwich line with ML417 in 1944. Flown by pilots of No 485 (Royal New Zealand Air Force) Sqn, it completed 69 fighter-bomber sweeps, 30 Normandy beach-head patrols and six armed reconnaissance sorties during the Allied landings. It accounted for two Junkers Ju 88s (one shared) and two Bf 109s downed and one damaged, one of the Ju 88s being shot down by its regular pilot F/O Johnnie Houlton over Omaha Beach on D-Day itself. ML407 served with six RNZAF, Polish, Free French and Norwegian squadrons of the 2nd Tactical Air Force in Normandy and Belgium, and was converted into a Tr9 trainer during 1951 for the Irish Air Corps. Acquired by Samuelson Films in 1968 as a back-up airframe for the film *The Battle of Britain* and later sold to the Strathallan Collection in Scotland, ML407 was bought in August 1979 by the late Nick Grace, and moved to his workshops in St Merryn, Cornwall, where he undertook a remarkable six-year rebuild with the help of former BBMF engineer Dick Melton. Flown again by Grace himself on 16 April 1985, ML407 incorporated some non-standard modifications during its reconstruction, including a lowered rear canopy with transparent 'tunnel' between the cockpits, and 'wet wing' fuel cells which increase capacity from 25 to 60 gallons per wing. Painted once again as a OU-V of No 485 (RNZAF) Sqn, ML407 was the centrepiece of a nostalgic re-union at St Just Aerodrome, Cornwall shortly after its re-birth when three of its former pilots, including Johnnie Houlton were re-united with their old mount

**These pages and overleaf** Another escapee from dereliction in Israel is Spitfire HF Mk IXE MJ730/G-BLAS, rescued by Robs Lamplough in 1979 and restored by Guy Black and Steve Atkins of Aero Vintage, and Trent Aero at East Midlands Airport. It is seen here aloft on a test flight from EMA in November 1988 with Rolls-Royce PLC's Dave Moore at the controls, painted as No 249 Sqn's GN-F for then owner American Fred Smith

**Left** Fred Smith never did take MJ730 across the Atlantic, but sold it in the UK to David Pennell. He chose a new colour scheme representing a presentation aircraft of No 154 Sqn, whose Spitfire Mk IXs operated in the Mediterranean during 1943/44

**Above** MJ730 correctly shows No 154 Sqn's badge – three arrows and a 'derestriction' road sign – but its motto is properly *His modis ad victoriam* (this way to victory). As classics students will know. *Nil illegitimae carborundum* means something entirely different

The Old Flying Machine Company's MH434/G-ASJV is perhaps the best known of all restored Spitfires thanks to exuberant airshow displays by the late Neil Williams and Ray Hanna (whose son Mark is at the controls here), and for the then record price of £260,000 paid for it at Christie's Duxford auction in 1983. MH434 is of 1943-vintage, built originally as a clip-wing LF Mk IX, but now in HF Mk IX guise with the two 20 mm cannon, four .303 Browning machine gun 'B' wing. Derived from the Spitfire Mk V to take advantage of the increased power available from the two-stage, two-speed supercharger Merlin 60-series engine, the Mk IX was developed in 1942 to counter the threat of the *Luftwaffe's* Fw 190 and was 70 mph faster than the Mk V, with a 10,000 foot increase in service ceiling. The Mark IX was the most-produced mark of Spitfire, with 5663 built, and to many pilots the best-handling of all

**These pages and overleaf** MH434 has a combat history. Flying this aircraft from RAF Hornchurch with No 222 (Natal) Sqn, Flt Lt H P Lardner-Burke, DFC shot down one Fw 190 and damaged another on 27 August 1943 while accompanying USAAF B-17 Fortresses on 'Ramrod' daylight escort duties, and brought down another Fw 190 and shared a Bf 109F the following month. After war service MH434 was sold to the Royal Netherlands Air Force and served in Indonesia before returning to Europe with the Belgian Air Force in 1953. On this photo sortie, flown by OFMC pilot Brian Smith, the aircraft had been painted in Belgian Air Force markings for the 1991 airshow season, when it took part in celebrations at the Biggin Hill Air Fair to mark the daring escape from Nazi-occupied Belgium in July 1941 of Lieutenant General Aviateur Baron 'Mike' Donnet, DFC. The code letters CK-D are spurious, a left-over from filming the television series *A Perfect Hero* during the previous year

**Above** MT719/I-SPIT wouldn't have found the grass so green and the
buttercups so yellow when on wartime service with No 17 Sqn operating out o
Vavuyina and China Bay during the Burma Campaign, commemorated by its
SEAC camouflage scheme. This Southampton-built LF Mk VIIIC stayed in the
East, joining the Indian Air Force at war's end, and was bought in 1978 by the
late Ormond Hayden-Baillie and his brother Wensley. Passed on to Italian
warbird enthusiast Franco Actis, it was restored in Turin by former BBMF
technicians Paul Mercer, 'Kick' Houltby and Pete Rushen, who installed a 1740
hp Merlin 114A engine from a Mosquito in place of its corroded Merlin 66, and
replaced some 90 per cent of its magnesium rivets during a four-year rebuild.
The BBMF's Sqn Ldr Paul Day performed the first flight from SIAI-Marchetti's
airfield at Vergiate on 27 October 1982. I-SPIT is now back in Britain in the
hands of Aircraft Investments and is maintained by Dick Melton. It is still
appropriately registered as G-VIII

# Better than new

**These pages and overleaf** In deepest Hampshire, not far from the Spitfire's Southampton birthplace and the numerous dispersal sites, mostly garages, in which components for some 8000 Spitfires were built in wartime, is the new 'Spitfire factory' set up by the late Charles Church and now operated by Dick Melton Aviation. In these views can be seen the camouflaged nose of Church's restored Tr9 PT462/GCTIX, and in yellow-etch primer finish his clip-wing LF Mk IXE PL344/G-IXCC, which saw active service with a number of 2nd TAF units during the Allied advance across occupied Europe in 1944/45. Left behind in the Netherlands at war's end to become an instructional airframe with the Anthony Fokker Technical School, it was retrieved by Charles Church (Spitfires) Ltd in 1985, and flew again after rebuild on 11 March 1991. Awaiting attention among the roof beams is the fuselage of former Indian Air Force Spitfire F Mk XIV SM832/G-WWII. Hurricane G-ORGI, undergoing the finishing touches to its rebuild by Paul Mercer when these pictures were taken, took to the air again on 8 September 1991, completing a busy year for Dick Melton Aviation

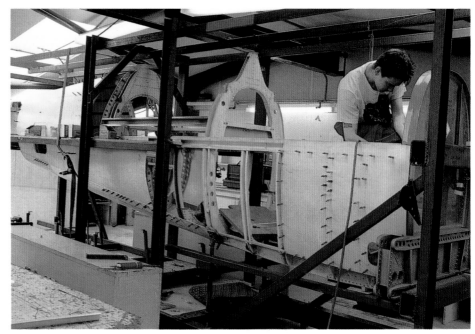

**Above** Dick Melton is also building up a post-production 509 Series Spitfire Trainer from newly fabricated components. When completed, it will be the 20,352nd Spitfire built

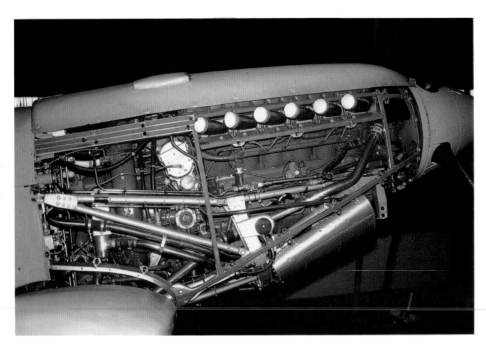

**Above** MJ627 now has an ex-Mosquito Merlin 76 installed; the engine ran again after rebuild on 18 March 1990

**Right** Almost there. Maurice Bayliss has been working on the restoration of his Spitfire Tr9 MJ627/G-BMSB since 1978. Built as an LF Mk IX at Castle Bromwich at the end of 1943, it was converted into a trainer for the Irish Air Corps eight years later. Following retirement and a spell of duty as an instructional airframe it came back to England in 1963 but found no takers when advertised for sale in *Flight International* at £1500! It was later bought for spares by the then owner of The Old Flying Machine Company's MH434/G-ASJV

**Above** Although one-off two-seat Spitfire conversions were carried out in the field by No 261 Sqn in Sicily and in Russia during World War 2, Vickers did not create a trainer variant of the fighter until 1946 when Mk VIII MT818 was rebuilt as the sole T Mk VIII N32/G-AIDN, which still survives in the United States. From it developed the tandem-seating Tr9 conversion which involved moving the front cockpit forward by $13\frac{1}{2}$ inches and adding a second cockpit behind, raised slightly to give the back-seater a reasonable forward view. Maurice Bayliss's Tr9 retains the Vickers canopy arrangement, which may be compared with ML407/G-LFIX's low-profile canopy and transparent inter-cockpit 'tunnel' illustrated in the previous chapter

**Right and overleaf** Being test flown by Mike Searle following rebuild by Trent Aero at East Midlands Airport is Warbirds of Great Britain's Spitfire LF Mk XVIE TE356/G-SXVI, one of a growing number of former RAF gate guardians to take to the air again. Delivered too late for wartime service, TE356 was downgraded to instructional airframe status in 1952 and spent 15 years on RAF Bicester's parade ground before Hollywood beckoned and it joined the non-flying 'extras' used in filming *The Battle of Britain*. Periods of 'pole sitting' outside the Central Flying School establishments at RAF Kemble, RAF Little Rissington and the RAF College at Cranwell followed. WoGB's Doug Arnold obtained the Spitfire in 1986 in trade for an ex-Yugoslav Air Force Republic P-47D Thunderbolt destined for the RAF Museum at Hendon. As G-SXVI the LF Mk XVIE flew again for the first time on 16 December 1987

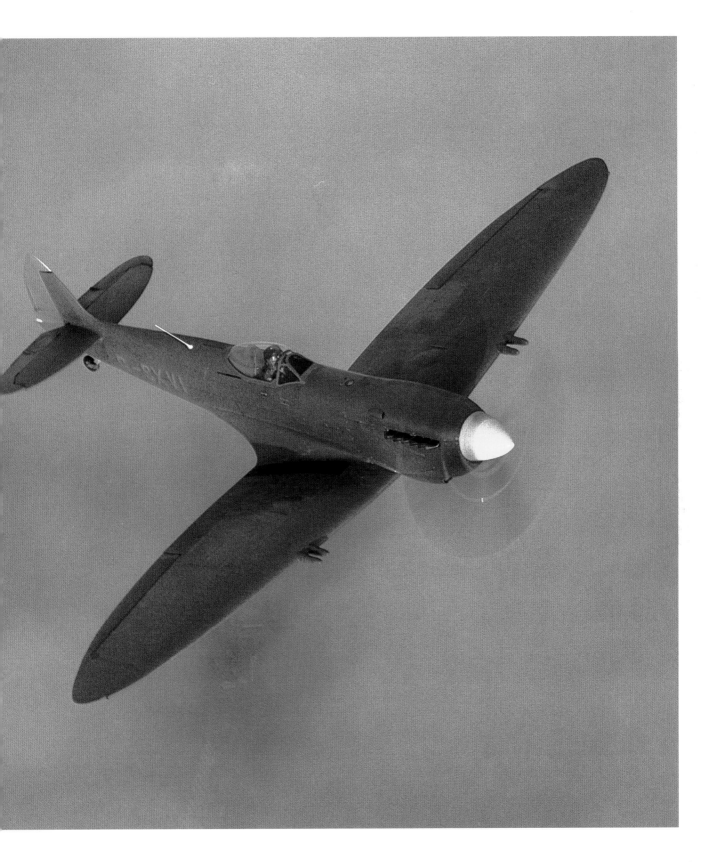

**Above** G-CDAN is also an LF Mk XVIE, a 'high-back' example this time. During service with No 17 Sqn at RAF Chivenor it appeared at the 1950 Farnborough Air Show (none too convincingly) disguised as a Messerschmitt Bf 109 for a Battle of Britain commemorative set-piece. Five years later it was in the hands of Metro-Goldwyn-Meyer as a 'prop' for filming cockpit scenes of *Reach for the Sky*, and later served as a source of spares for aircraft used in making *The Battle of Britain*. After many years of storage it was acquired by The Fighter Collection at Duxford. Stephen Grey is seen here giving the aircraft an air test in the autumn of 1988 prior to dismantling and shipping it to new owner Tim Wallis in New Zealand. Damaged in a landing accident shortly after arrival, it has since been rebuilt once more and now flies in original clip-winged configuration from Wanaka as TB863/ZK-XVI

**Above** BBMF and friends at Coningsby

**Right** Spitfire spinners. Three- four- and five-blade props lined up at the BBMF base at RAF Coningsby. In the foreground is the late Nick Grace's Tr9 ML407, and towards the rear – and definitely improperly dressed on parade – Spencer Flack's startlingly scarlet FR Mk XIVE G-FIRE/NH904, since sold in the US

Ten (count 'em) airworthy Spitfires
and two 'other brands' assembled at
the A&AEE Boscombe Down in
1990 for the Royal Air Force
Benevolent Fund's Battle of Britain
Salute. The BBMF's ill-fated
Hurricane LF363 GN-A heads the
line-up (right)

**Above** Spot the interloper. Spitfire and Hurricane flank a Spanish-built Hispano HA.1112-M1L Buchon painted up to represent a Messerschmitt Bf 109. At least it, like its adversaries, is Merlin-powered

**Left** Tails tell a tail. The early style rudder of The Old Flying Machine Company's MH434 gave way to the broad-chord, pointed-tip type (behind). Later in the Spitfire Mk IX production run, Griffon-engined variants (end of row) had an entirely different fin/rudder shape

**Above** *Scramble!* A young fighter pilot braves the machine gun fire of a strafing Messerschmitt to get airborne and beat off the attacking Hun. Actually this lad was having his dream of flying in a Spitfire fulfilled by BBC Television's *Jim'll Fix It*, whose director thought the ride in Nick Grace's two-seater would be further enlivened by an airfield attack from Lindsey Walton in his *Emil* look-alike Nord 1002/Messerschmitt Bf 108

**Above** Oberleutnant Lindsey von Walton eyes up the opposition prior to yet another dogfight in his *Luftwaffe*-decorated Nord 1002/Bf 108. Naturally, the dastardly 'Hun' always ends up going down in smoke. Lindsey, who farms quietly in rural Lincolnshire when not swooping out of the sun with gun muzzles flashing, reckons he holds the world record for being shot down yet surviving to fight another day

**Right** Spitfire designer Reginald Mitchell would have appreciated Concorde's cleanliness of line, but don't bet on which aircraft airshow-goers would choose as the better looking. This unique formation of The Old Flying Machine Company's and The Fighter Collection's Mk IXs and a British Airways Concorde was the show-stopping set-piece of the 1987 Biggin Hill Air Fair

Making its debut at the 1990 Biggin Hill Air Fair, the Spitfire Formation Aerobatic Team. Building on experience gained while filming the London Weekend Television series *A Piece of Cake*, Ray and Mark Hanna and fellow Old Flying Machine Company pilots Pete Jarvis and Carl Schofield worked up their unique routine flying the OFM's MH434, and Warbirds of Great Britain's LF Mk IXC/E NH238 (on right wing) and PR Mk XI PL983 (left wing). At the time it was thought that no Royal Air Force or any foreign service had ever put on a Spitfire formation aerobatic display in public, making this a unique occasion, but researchers later discovered that the French Air Force had fielded a trio of Mk IXCs as the *Patrouille Tricolore* from the *Ecole de Chasse* at Meknes, Morocco in 1947. Note original rounded rudders of MH434 and NH238, broad-chord pointed-tip style on the PR Mk XI